Conquering Shame

© 2023

By

LAKISHA FOXWORTH

CONTENTS

ACKNOWLEDGMENTS

With deepest gratitude, I first give thanks to God, whose strength continues to carry me through the journey of healing and whose grace sustains me each step of the way.

To every pastor, mentor, therapist, employer, friend, and family member who has embraced me with unwavering love and acceptance—your presence has been both an anchor and a light. The impact you've made on my life cannot be measured, only treasured.

I hold you in my heart with enduring appreciation and thank God upon every remembrance of you.

CHAPTER ONE

◦ ◇ ◦

What Is Shame, Really?

S hame is one of those emotions that sneaks in quietly but sticks around loudly. It tells us something is wrong with *us*, not just something we did. You might hear it in your mind saying things like, "I'm not good enough," "I'll never measure up," or "If they really knew me, they wouldn't love me."

Unlike guilt, which says, "I did something wrong," shame whispers, "I *am* something wrong." And that message can take root early in life and affect how we see ourselves for years to come.

In the Bible, we see the first mention of shame in the Garden of Eden. Adam and Eve were created to live in freedom, fully seen and loved by God. They were naked and unashamed. But after they disobeyed God, they immediately felt exposed, embarrassed, and afraid. So they hid. That's what shame does-it makes us want to hide.

Instead of running to God with their mistake, they ran from Him. How many times have we done the same? Maybe you've messed up and thought, "God doesn't want to hear from me." But what if they had been honest with Him? What if they had said, "We messed up, and we're sorry"? We don't know what would've happened, but it shows us how powerful honesty and connection can be in healing shame.

We also experience shame through how we're raised. When we're toddlers, we start figuring out, "Is it okay to be me?" If we're encouraged and supported, we grow in confidence. But if we're criticized, controlled, or ignored, we may start to believe we're not enough. That message can stick with us into adulthood.

Shame affects how we show up in the world. It can make us feel small, quiet our voices, and stop us from pursuing things we love. But here's the good news: the opposite of shame is joy, confidence, respect, and freedom. And that's what God wants for you.

Jesus said in John 10:10 that He came so we could have life-real life-and have it abundantly. That includes freedom from shame.

You were never meant to live in hiding. You were created to live in truth, love, and purpose.

In the next chapters, we'll explore how shame shows up in our emotions, our bodies, and our relationships-and most importantly, how to overcome it.

CHAPTER TWO

◇ ◇ ◇

Where Does Shame Come From?

S hame doesn't just appear out of nowhere-it's something we learn. It grows from our earliest experiences, especially in how people responded to us when we were young.

Maybe you were told to "stop crying" or "toughen up." Or perhaps you were compared to a sibling, ignored, or made to feel like a burden. These messages may not have been said out loud, but we felt them in how we were treated. Over time, those small moments can plant deep roots of shame.

As children, we're like sponges-we soak up what's around us. We look to adults to understand who we are and if we're loved. If the adults in our lives were safe, kind, and consistent, we likely learned that we matter. But if they were harsh, unavailable, or unpredictable, we might have started believing something was wrong with us.

Even good parents can unintentionally pass down shame. If a child is constantly corrected without being encouraged, they might begin to think they're bad, not just that they made a mistake.

And it's not just about parents. Shame can come from teachers, coaches, church leaders, or even friends. Any place where we expected love or safety-but instead felt judged or rejected-can leave a mark.

Trauma can also create deep shame. If you've been abused, neglected, or hurt in ways that made you feel powerless, you might carry shame that was never yours to begin with. That's not your fault.

What someone did to you doesn't define who you are. Sometimes shame is cultural or generational. In some families or communities, showing emotion is seen as weakness. In others, being different or standing out is discouraged. These messages teach us to hide our true selves just to feel accepted.

But here's the truth: you were never meant to live covered in shame. The painful things that happened to you don't get the final say. You have the power to unlearn shame and replace it with love, truth, and confidence.

The first step is understanding where your shame began. As we move forward, we'll explore how those early messages affect your body, your emotions, and your relationships-and how you can start to heal.

CHAPTER THREE

◇ ◇ ◇

How Shame Affects Your Body and Emotions

S hame doesn't just live in our thoughts-it settles into our bodies and emotions too. You might not even realize how much it's affecting you until you start paying attention.

Have you ever felt your stomach twist when someone criticizes you? Or your heart race when you're about to speak in a group? That's not just nervousness-it can be shame showing up in your body. Shame triggers the same "fight, flight, or freeze" response as danger. Your brain says, "Uh-oh, I'm not safe," and your body responds to protect you. You might shrink back, avoid eye contact, slouch your shoulders, or feel your face flush. It's your body's way of saying, "Hide."

Emotionally, shame can make us feel small, unworthy, or even invisible. It can lead to:

- Anxiety ("I'm always afraid I'll mess up.")

- Depression ("I don't feel good about myself.")

- Anger ("If I push people away, they can't hurt me.")

- Numbness ("I don't feel anything at all anymore.")

Sometimes, we don't realize we're feeling shame-we just know we're exhausted, anxious, or disconnected. But when we dig deeper, we often find that old, hidden message: "I'm not good enough."

Here's the good news: your body also remembers safety, love, and joy. Just like shame taught your nervous system to hide, healing can teach it to come back to peace.

Practices like deep breathing, grounding exercises, and gentle movement can help your body learn to feel safe again. Talking with someone you trust-a friend, therapist, or spiritual mentor-can begin to calm your inner storm.

You are not broken. Your emotions aren't bad. They're clues. And your body isn't betraying you-it's trying to protect you based on old experiences. The more you understand what's happening inside, the more power you have to choose healing.

In the next chapter, we'll explore how shame affects your spirit-and how God invites you into restoration and truth.

CHAPTER FOUR

◇ ◈ ◇

How Shame Affects Your Spirit

S hame doesn't just affect your thoughts and feelings-it can also affect your spirit. It makes you question your worth, your identity, and even your relationship with God.

Many people carry spiritual shame without realizing it. Maybe you were told you had to be perfect to be accepted. Or maybe you feel like you've made too many mistakes for God to love you. Shame whispers, "You're too far gone," "You're not spiritual enough," or "You should be better by now."

But that's not the voice of God. That's the voice of shame.

In Scripture, God is always drawing people closer-not pushing them away. From the Garden of Eden to the cross, we see a God who comes toward us in our brokenness. Jesus didn't avoid the hurting, the outcast, or the ashamed. He reached for them. He restored them. He loved them.

Shame tries to convince us that God's love is conditional. But Romans 8:38-39 reminds us that nothing-absolutely nothing-can separate us from His love. Not our failures. Not our past. Not even our doubts.

When you live under spiritual shame, prayer feels hard. Worship feels distant. You might even stop showing up altogether because you think you're not "worthy" enough. But here's the truth: you're already loved. You don't have to earn it. You just have to receive it.

Healing from spiritual shame means allowing yourself to be honest with God. He already knows what you're carrying. And He's not mad at you-He wants to walk with you through it.

Start by being honest in your prayers. You don't need fancy words. Just tell Him what's really going on in your heart. Let Him remind you who you are: chosen, loved, and not alone.

In the next chapter, we'll talk about how shame affects our relationships-and how to stop it from keeping you disconnected from others.

CHAPTER FIVE

◇ ◇ ◇

Shame and Your Relationships

S hame doesn't just stay inside of us-it spills into our relationships. It changes how we connect with people, how we let them in (or don't), and how safe we feel being fully seen.

When we carry shame, we often believe we're not worthy of love, so we put up walls. Or we try to prove our worth by being perfect, helpful, or always agreeable-even if it costs us our peace.

Shame can show up as:

- People-pleasing ("If I keep everyone happy, they won't rejectme.")
- Isolation ("If I stay away, I can't get hurt.")
- Control ("If I stay in charge, I won't feel powerless.")
- Defensiveness ("If I admit I'm wrong, they'll think I'm a failure.")

In friendships, shame might make you afraid to be honest. In marriage, it might lead to feeling misunderstood or unworthy of your partner's love. In parenting, you may pass on the shame you haven't healed from yourself. And in church or community, you might wear a mask because you're afraid people would judge the "real you."

But real connection only happens when we allow ourselves to be seen. That's scary-but it's also where healing lives.

Healthy relationships are built on:

- Safety: I can be myself without fear.
- Honesty: I can speak the truth with love.
- Boundaries: I don't have to overextend to be valued.
- Grace: I'm allowed to grow and make mistakes.

You don't have to earn love. You don't have to be perfect to belong. The right people will honor your healing journey, not shame you for it.

And if shame has affected your relationships, there's still time to make things right. Start with one honest conversation. Ask for support. Apologize when needed. Receive love when it's given. You're worth connection-not just surviving in silence.

In the next chapter, we'll explore how shame impacts your relationship with yourself-and how to learn to love the person you see in the mirror.

CHAPTER SIX

◇ ◇ ◇

Your Relationship with Yourself

One of the most powerful but overlooked effects of shame is how it shapes the way you see yourself. Long before we try to change how others treat us, we have to look at how we treat ourselves. Shame can turn our inner voice into a harsh critic. You might find yourself thinking things like: - "I'm so stupid."

"Why can't I get it right?"

"I'll never be good enough."

Over time, those thoughts become your normal. You stop questioning them and start believing them.

But would you say those things to a friend? Would you call someone you love a failure? Of course not. So why talk to yourself that way?

Learning to relate to yourself with kindness is a huge part of healing. It doesn't mean pretending everything is fine. It means telling yourself the truth-with grace.

Try replacing those harsh thoughts with gentler ones:

Instead of "I'm so stupid," say, "I made a mistake, but I'm stilllearning."

Instead of "Why can't I get it right?" say, "I'm growing, and thattakes time."

Instead of "I'll never be good enough," say, "I am already worthyof love and respect."

You are not your past. You are not your pain. You are a whole person, made in God's image, with the capacity to heal and grow. You don't have to wait until you're "fixed" to be kind to yourself. Start now. Celebrate small wins. Forgive yourself when you fall short. Rest when you're tired. Speak life over yourself-even if it feels awkward at first.

Self-compassion is not weakness. It's strength in motion. And it's one of the most powerful tools you have for breaking the cycle of shame.

In the final chapter, we'll talk about practical ways to start walking in freedom-one step at a time.

CHAPTER SEVEN

◇ ◇ ◇

Practical Tools for Healing Shame

ealing from shame isn't about having one big breakthrough. It's a journey-step by step, choice by choice. You've already begun that journey by learning more about shame and how it has impacted your life. Now, let's talk about what you can *do* to keep moving forward.

Here are some practical tools to help you heal:

Name It to Tame It

When you feel that heavy, "not good enough" feeling, pause and name it. Say, "This is shame." Just calling it out begins to loosen its grip.

Challenge the Lies

Shame feeds on silence and secrecy. When you hear thoughts like "I'm unlovable" or "I'll never change," ask yourself, "Is that true-or is that shame talking?" Replace lies with truth.

Practice Self-Compassion

Speak to yourself with kindness. When you mess up, say, "I'm still learning." When you're tired, say, "I deserve rest." Be the voice of grace in your own mind.

Connect with Safe People

Find a therapist, mentor, or trusted friend who can walk with you. Healing happens in safe relationships. Let others remind you of your worth when you forget.

Engage in Healing Practices

This could be journaling, prayer, worship, grounding exercises, or body movement like walking or stretching. These small habits help your nervous system feel safe again.

Revisit God's Truth About You

Return often to Scripture. You are fearfully and wonderfully made (Psalm 139:14). You are loved, chosen, and redeemed (Ephesians 1:4-7). God is not ashamed of you-He's pursuing you with love.

Set Boundaries with Shame

When shame tries to take over, speak back. Say, "I hear you, but I don't agree with you." You don't have to believe every thought that comes into your mind.

Remember, healing takes time. Some days will feel lighter than others. But every time you show up for yourself, you are reclaiming your story. You're not walking in shame-you're walking in strength.

In the final section, we'll reflect on how far you've come and the freedom that lies ahead.

CONCLUSION

◇ ◇ ◇

Walking in Freedom
You've come a long way.

You've taken a brave journey through the roots of shame, how it affects your body, your heart, your faith, your relationships-even the way you see yourself. And maybe, along the way, something in you started to shift. Maybe you saw yourself with a little more compassion. Maybe you found words for things you couldn't name before. That's healing. And that's courage.

Let's be clear: shame will try to come back. But now, you have the tools to recognize it and respond differently. You don't have to hide anymore. You don't have to pretend you're okay when you're not.

You don't have to carry the weight of lies that never belonged to you.

You are loved. You are valuable. You are not alone.

You don't have to be perfect to be free. You just have to keep choosing truth over shame, love over fear, and healing over hiding-one day at a time.

God is not ashamed of you. He's proud of the steps you're taking. He's walking with you in every hard conversation, every quiet prayer, every moment you choose to show up instead of shut down.

So take a breath. Lift your head. The journey continues, and you are not who you used to be.

You are seen. You are known. You are whole. And you are free.

Shame Awareness Quiz & Coping Strategies

◇ ◇ ◇

This quiz will help you identify how shame may be showing up in your life, followed by practical strategies to begin healing.

Awareness Quiz

❖ Do you often feel like you're not good enough, even when others say otherwise?

❖ Do you tend to replay mistakes or past failures in your mind?

❖ Do you avoid certain people, places, or conversations out of fear of judgment?

❖ Do you have a hard time accepting compliments or praise?

❖ Do you struggle with perfectionism or feel like you always have to prove yourself?

❖ Do you often compare yourself to others and feel less than?

❖ Do you feel the need to hide parts of your story or personality?

❖ Do you experience anxiety when being vulnerable or honest about your feelings?

❖ Do you feel like you need to earn love, approval, or acceptance?

❖ Do you avoid asking for help because it makes you feel weak or like a burden?

Scoring: For each question you answered 'Yes,' place a checkmark. The more you check, the more shame may be influencing your thoughts, behaviors, and self-worth.

Coping Strategies for Healing Shame

1. **Practice Self-Compassion** - Speak to yourself with the same kindness you'd offer a close friend.

2. **Identify Shame Triggers** - Notice when you feel small, not enough, or tempted to hide. What triggered it?

3. **Journal Your Thoughts** - Write out what you're feeling and gently challenge the shame messages.

4. **Use Grounding Techniques** - Deep breathing, body scans, or mindful movement can help regulate your nervous system.

5. **Replace Shame with Truth** - Create a list of affirmations or scriptures that remind you of your worth.

6. **Talk with Safe People** - Share your story with someone who won't judge you. Shame grows in silence but dies in safe connection.

7. **Create a Shame-Free Zone -** Make space in your life where you're allowed to rest, mess up, and be human without fear of judgment.

8. **Reconnect with God -** Spend quiet time praying, reflecting, or simply being present with the One who loves you unconditionally.

Affirmation of Freedom from Shame

◇ ◇ ◇

Today, I choose to release the shame that has weighed me down.

I am not my past mistakes.

I am not defined by the opinions of others.

I am loved, worthy, and enough.

I was created with purpose and intention.

God delights in me and has a plan for my abundant life.

I embrace my true identity: honored, accepted, and free.

I walk forward today in truth, healing, and hope.

Shame has no hold on me.

I am who God says I am.

I am free.

About the Author

◇ ◇ ◇

Lakisha Foxworth, LMFT

Lakisha Foxworth, LMFT, is a licensed marriage and family therapist, author, and ordained minister with a passion for helping others break free from the grip of shame and emotional pain. With over a decade of experience in mental health and spiritual care, Lakisha empowers individuals to heal, grow, and embrace their God-given identity.

Through her private practice, Grace Inspired Counseling Services, she provides compassionate, faith-centered therapy to those navigating anxiety, trauma, life transitions, and relational challenges. Known for her warm, relatable style and deep insight, Lakisha creates safe spaces for others to rediscover their worth and walk in truth.

In Conquering Shame, she offers a powerful blend of clinical wisdom, biblical encouragement, and personal reflection to guide readers on a journey from hidden pain to healing freedom.

When she's not counseling or writing, Lakisha enjoys quiet moments of reflection, creative expression, and spending time with loved ones. She resides in South Florida and continues to inspire others to live whole, free, and fully seen.

References

Brown, B. (2012). *Daring greatly: How the courage to be vulnerable transforms the way we live, love, parent, and lead*. Gotham Books.

Erikson, E. H. (1950). *Childhood and society*. Norton.

Neff, K. (2011). *Self-compassion: The proven power of being kind to yourself*. William Morrow.

The Holy Bible, New International Version. (2011). Zondervan. (Original work published 1978)

The Holy Bible, New King James Version. (1982). Thomas Nelson.

www.ingramcontent.com/pod-product-compliance
Lightning Source LLC
Chambersburg PA
CBHW061758040426
42447CB00011B/2365